BOOKS BY ROD McKUEN

And Autumn Came
Stanyan Street and Other Sorrows
Listen to the Warm
Lonesome Cities
Twelve Years of Christmas
In Someone's Shadow

in someone's shadow

in
someone's
shadow

ROD McKUEN

CHEVAL BOOKS

Distributed by Random House, Inc.

New York

This Is a Book for The Kid

A friend is a person with whom I may be sincere. Before him, I may think aloud.

Emerson

One need only ask to Receive — anon.

contents

ANOTHER BEGINNING

for Jerry Kramer

One day a man will take you on the high roads;
After a time he'll leave you someplace nice
or tell you where the big boys play.
They usually string out their games
      in someone's shadow.
   It could be yours.
More likely mine,
for mine's grown longer and there's more room here.

I ache to learn some new games now,
      I've been away from town too long.
To see a new door open I'd go almost anywhere.
Even backward,
if I thought I had the time.

I'm mad at midnight
        for the things it didn't do,
that doesn't mean I wouldn't take a chance again.

Few angels have been heard to sing
but many purr when stroked just so.

Lie down and leave your imprint in the sand,
my hand will trace it into everything I need.
That's how reality begins,
        shadows made something real
or reality turned back into a shadow.
I need the sureness of the shadow world again.
To make me whole.

in someone's shadow

If I am anything at all
I'm what I've gotten out of sand.
Not only that washed in
    from seas and islands
but any piece of earth
    (however small)
a man can hold
securely in his hand.

Catch me in the sunlight.
Catch me pacing past the trees.
Build a fence around me
the moment that you see me running.
I'm so elusive sometimes
I miss the things worth stopping for.

I need.

Not more trees.
Not more rain in back-yard barrels
        or racing down the gutters to the drain.

I need the comfort
of a friendly back or belly.
Seen sometimes in magazines
or made up in my mind.

You know the ones I mean
They shout out at you like the trees in April
Or blossom on you like strawberry smiles.

I have been assaulted by soft smiles at a distance.
The way some radios attack you from across the room
when you're strapped up in a barber chair.
The way you're raped by Muzak in an elevator.

in someone's shadow

Now comes the time for closeness once again.
Turn me over gently.
Hold me for the man I am.
Smooth out the wrinkles on my face
And love me—please.
Because I need.

The big boys play
in someone's shadow down the street
and I'm detached.

That's as it should be,
for I need more than games.

Take a chance on me.
I haven't any name
but what you'll give me when you leave.

IN SOMEONE'S SHADOW

One | ENCOUNTERS

March 31

I'll ring up one day
and you may wonder who I am.

I too might not be quite so sure
if you're the one who smelled like violets
      or left my shoulder tatooed with a bite
that took three weeks to go away.
Or the one who, going down the stairs,
turned back long enough to say
Don't call me after ten o'clock
my mother goes to bed quite early.

Those of us who think that *need*
and *night* are both the same
have so many little scraps of paper
stuffed in wallets and tucked up under books
or safely put away in dresser drawers.

Names and numbers scribbled
on the backs of business cards
or finely printed on old matchbook covers.

I never have the guts to throw them out.
                    Do you?

I suppose
that like a pilgrim
I keep imagining my colony of cards
can one day be called up
to form a fort against the need to walk.

I must remember from now on
to write beside their names *thin shoulderblades*
or *this one had a mole along the left side of her stomach.*
Some identifying thing
so when I go to make those calls
I'll know just who I'm calling.

But
saving little scraps of paper
and knowing they'll remain just that,
not transferred into address books
        or indexed in a file,
is a kind of mental masturbation
                        good to no one.

Not even those of us who think
the inside side of matchbook covers
        with a penciled number
is a kind of life insurance
can expect a proper settlement
when the accident
of being with our own selves only
overtakes us in an alleyway
or a bedroom.

April 5

Life goes slow without love.
It moves along unhurried.
The sun rises.
          The sun goes down.

There are those who pass by
changing the time-cycle
if you're willing to wait.

I am always shy
with these journeymen at first
and by the time I get to know them
they've gone away.

April 6

I have learned no new alphabet this week.
No new yardstick different from the last time out.
The old language has had to do too long a time.
I use the past arithmetic
       to make the present work.
Yet even going from room to room
I walk with arms outstretched.

April 12

We come into the world alone.
              We go away the same.
We're meant to spend the interlude between
                              in closeness
              Or so we tell ourselves.
But it's a long way from the morning to the evening.

Two | NO WHISKY BARS

May 5

The sky
is the forehead of the morning
passing the sun along the day,
distributing the clouds
that move above us
and ride with us till nightfall.

And your eyes
are the bottom of the day
set on fire by words,
made to move by sighs
and the rustling of the trees.

We'll go to the hills then,
            take our time.
Climb until we find one
    closest to the sky.

I'll spread a blanket on the ground
and make a picnic of your body.
You'll face the sky and count the clouds
and when the counting stops
I'll take you home again,
down a dozen hills under a hundred skies.

I know the ground is not yet green all over
            but trust me.
I'll find the greenest hill of all
and your red dress will be the single flower
that grows against the grass.

Me and the day
we care for you
without the rivalry of common lovers
and we'll be careful as the rain,
            gentle as the clouds.

May 17

I believe that crawling into you
is going back into myself.
That by the act of
joining hands with you
I become more of me.

There are no whisky bars
for dancers like ourselves,
and so we move into each other
like drunkards into open doorways.

My need for you is near addiction.

No sailor ever had tattoos
growing on his forearm
the way your smile
has willed itself back behind my eyes.

It will not dissolve.
It will not divide.
For I am nothing if not you.

May 18

Awakened by the bells this morning
      I got up early.
You didn't know it
but the birds that marched along the beach
were chanting out a Sunday love mass.

I let you sleep because I love to watch you
all disheveled and unwound
dressed up in your undress like a careless animal
your hair uncovered
unmanned by anyone but me.
Forgive me if I leave you while you sleep.
I forgive you for not knowing.

I'll walk the beach now limp and not so lonely.
Then crawling back where I belong
   (even as the sun comes up)
I'll fall asleep again down your shadow.

in someone's shadow

May 24

Spring will chase us
through the summer into fall
and find us beached upon some snowy shore
waiting for the spring to come again.

Then gingerly we'll go through jonquils
to seek out other summers.

Birthday to birthday,
         season to season,
every hour will be an anniversary
                  of the hour just past.

May 25

There are some forests that I haven't known.
Some tree trunks I've never wrapped my legs around
                                        and climbed.
A million branches I might have slid down
                had I had the time.

Still
some leaves trembled in the wood and caught my ear.
Some twigs beneath the hooves of deer snapped
                and signaled *spring,*
waking me from endless winter thoughts.

in someone's shadow

May 26

I'd rather be without a woman
than know a God I couldn't trust.
That's why I pray with caution
till I'm sure.

I gave myself to myself only
for so long a time
I've had to be led back
     to God and women too,
          step
             by
                step.

Now halfway home
it's time I knelt down
on the asphalt once again
and prayed for more than daily bread.

May 29

If you don't come back to bed
I'll fall asleep and dream up Rousseau's lion,
leaving you in your own kitchen jungle.

Let the dishes wait.

Come to bed and bring a cup of milk
in case the cat gets hungry in the night.

June 1

Your perfume's not as dangerous as your shoulders
                              you needn't try so hard.
You only have to look at me
          that's all.
Or turn while walking down the stairs below me.

Don't blacken up your eyes
or I'll be bad and make you cry—
then every time I look at you
I'll think about the black girl in Bimini.
                         Funny,
she never drew white lines around *her* eyebrows.
She must have been content to be herself.

The only lipstick you should use is love.

June 15

Hurry.
Sunday will not wait,
even for a woman.

The ships are in the harbor
        and to catch up now
        we'll have to steal a little time from God
(hard to do with our accounts so overdrawn).

Hurry up.

June 29

Who will keep the brown days turning
            when we go?
It's hard to picture all their moving parts
functioning without our hands to turn them.

The mechanics of *maybe* might not work
without an audience of two or more
that's why I never worry over rain.

The flood would never sweep our house away
for who'd be left to watch the sunset
            when we're gone?

June 30

There is no wrong side
   or right side.

No misery in not being loved,
   only in not loving.

I learned these truths myself
to tell them to you now,
as you go sailing through the sun
   on your way toward life.

July 4

I've come to know your body and your eyes
the way a child might memorize
        his favorite fairy tale.
Yet I need the reading once a night
the same as children do.

Don't leave out one dragon
or a single tree that grows within the forest
that the Knight rides through.

So a child will tell you
of the story he loves best.

Leave your body as it was this afternoon
            or yesterday.
                    Changing nothing.
I think I know the way it floats above the bed
            on summer afternoons
and dives into electric blankets in the winter.
Still I must be sure my memory hasn't made
new freckles your beach-brown shoulders never knew.

July 5

Once I wrote a song
                     almost.
Sixteen lines that walked
up from my belly to my head.

As I stood waiting for the light to change
        and making up a melody,
     a yellow bus passed by—slowly.
Looking up I lost the lines I thought I'd learned
             and several more that never came
all because a bus passed by
and someone smiled from out a yellow window.

Buses pass by seldom
and horsemen not at all
I couldn't crib or fake your shoulders
        if I once forgot
and so each time I hold you
I test myself again.

in someone's shadow

July 11

If you gave me children
        one or ten,
I couldn't love you more.
             Less maybe.
For I have only love enough for you.
It takes the middle and both ends
of all the love I've got
to keep you safe.

Children, then,
and birds and trees
and summer afternoons
will have to be my good friends only.
For I'm as selfish with my love
as you are with your body
in the morning.

July 12

Don't sit that way.
Your tears fall on your breasts
like raindrops on the window ledge
and I'm reduced to nothing
but a trouble-maker
in a Barcelona chair.
If I want tears
I'll wind the phonograph
and let it do my crying for me.

Women use their tears like poison darts.
We're not at war with *love*.
If I've been drafted once again,
I'll pack a bag for Canada.

July 14

I wrote Paul this morning
after reading his poem,
     I told him,
it's ok to drop your pants
to old men sometimes
but I wouldn't recommend it
     as a way of life.

I didn't mail the letter.

We're all falling
we never learn about it
　　　till we land.

Paul might fall a different way
but who's to say which way is better
　　　till they've been there
　　and come back safe.

　　　　　　　　　　in someone's shadow

July 15

I have no journeys
that I care to make just now
      unless it's to the middle of the bed
     (and then I'd own it all).

Where were you last night/never mind.
       The room is warmer now.

July 16

Years from now we may not need to touch so often
       or roll together in the sand
or eat each other with our eyes.

It could be time will make it easy
to go together side by side
with not a single bedroom thought.

But now the elevator man nodding at you
as we step inside his four-by-four castle
makes me worry more than generals worry
when they lose a war.

August 5

Down the cliffs we go to Marshall Beach,
        stumbling
            smiling,
                    single
                    file.

With your skirts above your knees
you bring back can-can dancers
    from the Moulin Rouge.

Make the old men happy, little girl,
keep your skirts up high.
Give them more than summer sunshine
to fill their empty lives.

One day twenty years from now
I might join the beach-front line myself.
I hope the young girls will be just as nice to me.

August 6

The sea gets hungry every August
tired of eating only rivers.
So when the glances end on shore
     take your ankles to the water.

There's a circus turning round somewhere
beyond the summer beach
     we'll wade along the shoreline
          to the ferris wheel
     and kick some stars tonight.

Just for now
let the ocean see your ankles.
The waves are clumsy but they're kind.
              Me too.

in someone's shadow

August 7

There will be revolutions
we can touch one day
instead of only those
that timidly touch us.

Revolutions made in fold-down beds
that slide into the closet
                    from the guilty day.
Rallys done for freedom
    from the fear of those
        who try their best
            to push us from
                each other.

Then I'll vote Republican
and you'll be older too
and both of us will try
to walk our children
through the world
          we've just come through.

They'll protest as we have done
that their lives are theirs.
And they'll be just as right as we are now.

But every generation gap
          should have some kind of bridge
     even if it's only made of love.

Three | KNOWING WHEN TO LEAVE

August 27

Hello,
I'm here.

I got through one more night
of jacking off and late late shows
               and sleeping pills
your doctor had prescribed for *you*.

I've arrived again
          to turn your coffee on
and feed your cat
          and take your last night's garbage out
and other menial tasks,
like making love to you
before you've had your morning bath.

How like that regiment of men
who've passed down through your life
                    I must be.
You crack the whip
as though you've had a ten-year practice,
barking your commands
like the whispered sighs of love.
I'll never break the chain
though I might rattle it
                    from time to time.

I wouldn't call my life with you submissive,
it's nothing more than giving back
some of the hope I get from you sometimes
            when we're making love
                    or eating popcorn at the movies
and you smile at me and not the pictures.

Still, I'll go softly
when it's time to go
and not wake up the neighbor's dog downstairs.

I'm good at exits.
I leave them laughing like Durante would.

I never fight back any more,
        though that's what we all want,
a fight that proves we've each been wronged.

I've learned that when love goes
there is no one you can blame
unless it was The Book of Job
        or Whatshisname.

September 19

Kelly, lying on his back
      his feet up in the air,
looks too uncomfortable to be asleep.
Yet what man or animal would dare
to be so vulnerable awake?

If we could once let down the guards
there might be other animals
who'd look us over more than once.

Up to your hips in love you lead me on
through bedrooms when it pleases you.
Up to our hearts in lies
we seldom venture past the parlor to tomorrow.

October 3

If you had listened hard enough
you might have heard
        what I meant to say.

    Nothing.

October 7

When we've finally learned to love
who'll teach us how to hate again?
And what will we begin
to break down first,
our bodies or our friends?

Like cats that claw
amid the chaos of new garbage
will we become adept at hate,
good enough to call ourselves professionals?

Or will we go like gypsy vagabonds
seeking out new targets every night?

October 14

It will be a Charles Ives winter.
You can tell that even now
by the way the branches tremble after dark
and the wind rakes up the leaves,
saving the rain the trouble.

I've not yet become an expert on myself
though I thought I was a time or two.
But I'm willing to drop my mirror for a while
and hold yours up to you.

I have the winter just beyond the hill
to help me.
     It will be a Charles Ives winter,
     full of holidays
           for some.

Four | WINTER

January 3

The moon rose over the town tonight
like the warm round belly of a young girl,
exposed so all might see and compliment it.

Alone in the public park
I watched it edge above tall buildings
and climb through clouds
till it was time to journey down again
behind the trees.

The show over,
a girl stopped and asked my name.
            I kept on walking.

in someone's shadow

January 11

Mr. Kelly barks at shadows now;
that's a habit he'll have to break.
For shadows offer all the safety
left in life.

I dare not think what might replace
the shadows that I've had to learn to love,
but I stand ready one more time
to learn a new geography
if that becomes a necessary thing to do.

Meanwhile
there's a certain sureness
in the dark parts of the house,
for you're still hiding there.

January 17

When we've long forgotten why
I came back to San Francisco by myself
and why you went away alone
    and why you smiled at me
            the first time ever.
There will still be little things
our memories will keep,
some things known to each other only.

I cannot speculate
on what our cluttered mind will save—
            sleepy Sundays,
or a nosebleed after love.

I know only the dying heart
needs the nourishment of memory
to live beyond too many winters.

January 18

I've put these few things down
to help remind me of a year
when love was plentiful as table wine
and warm as Mr. Kelly's back
when he lies next to me at night
grumbling at imaginary fleas.

I've set the corner posts in only.
The fence will be a different one
than what it really was
but it will be the best
that wishing thoughts can build.

When I've memorized the words
I'll go out looking once again.

Later,
lying close in someone's shadow
I'll call back all the times
you danced off from the bedroom
          in your underwear
and brought back mugs of coffee,
the way a Bible temptress
might have brought back baskets of fine fruit
          for Solomon.

You always thought me sleeping.
                    No.
I woke up first,
just to see you stumbling
from the bedroom half-awake
blind eyes searching for the kitchen.

Just to be awake when you awakened me.

FOUR POEMS FROM
A MAN ALONE

for Frank Sinatra

EMPTY IS

Empty is
the sky before the sun wakes up the morning.
The eyes of animals in cages.
            The faces of women mourning
            when everything has been taken
                                    from them.

Me?
            Don't ask me about empty.

Empty is a string of dirty days
held together by some rain
and the cold wind drumming
    at the trees again.

Empty is the color of the fields
along about September
when the days go marching
in a line toward November.

Empty is the hour before sleep
kills you every night
then pushes you to safety
    away from every kind of light.

            Empty is me.
    Empty is me.

SOME TRAVELING MUSIC

How can you say something new
          about being alone?
Tell someone you're a loner
and right away they think you're lonely.

It's not the same thing, you know.

It's not wanting to put all your marbles
          in one pocket.
It's caring enough not to care too much.

Mostly it's letting yourself come first for a while.

NIGHT

I can just about get through the day
but the night makes me nervous.
      Not for any reason
except maybe that it catches you unaware
and follows you the way a woman follows
when she wants something.

I've been in every kind of night
so I shouldn't be afraid of darkness
but still the night makes me nervous.

OUT BEYOND THE WINDOW

My window looks out over the park.
    Every year I've moved another story up,
till now I'm almost close enough
      to the roof of the sky
        to touch it.

I could even move the clouds aside
      but no clouds come.
If they did I'd welcome them,
for I have few visitors here any more.

There must be roads somewhere,
      highways I haven't found.
Something more than clouds
out beyond the window.

DID YOU SAY
THE WAR IS OVER?

FARMING

Who made those wars romantic in the first place?
Who led us down the line in patriotism's name,
filling us with King and Country, Fatherland and Flag,
Telling us to die was beautiful?

Who told us that as huddled masses yearning to *break* free
we'd have to kill a man for every foot of ground we gained?
The path we've cleared is now a freeway.
Passing through so many ill-kept fields.

Guns make lousy plowshares
But oh they rust so beautifully.
Think of how they'd look
With snap beans crawling over them.

for Mike Wallace

THE PRINCIPLES OF ARCHITECTURE

The young can save the world I think
      by growing older in a hurry.
We need a whole new age of older men
          in brand-new vests.
If we're to know again the dignity of tall men,
then all those who are running in the streets
          with rocks and bricks
had better learn to use their stones
to build foundations, not to slice off roofs.

You build by pulling down the rubble.
But first you have to have a plan.

for Sister Mark Sandy

ELECTION

I used to wonder why
God only came to visit me on Sunday.
He must have been as bored with me
        as I with him.
One hour once a week was once enough.

God's really hurt nobody but the poor
and still they go on voting every year.
        An echo not a choice.

I'll deal with death when it comes knocking,
        the same is true with God.

Even I don't practice what I preach.
If I believed there were no God
I'd have to face the possibility of no me.

DID YOU SAY THE WAR IS OVER?

Did you say the war is over
and we're pulling out?
It means we'll have more manpower
                      here at home
          to burn down schools.

That yellow country made good testing ground
                  for napalm on the campus.

Let's see the chancellors resist the new democracy
with their caps and gowns ablaze.

What troubled times we live in
what days of strife and stress,
even kindergarten kids
are given to unrest.

The acne of perfection now must be
to punch the teacher in the nose
        who gave you F instead of D.

SOUP

It troubles me
that there are those
who want their kind of freedom bad enough
to take away their neighbors' in the process.

I nurse my wounds in private
and when the bandages get sour
I put them in a private garbage bin.
Why contaminate my neighbor and his city?

Voting is not as easy as it used to be.
You always wind up electing somebody.

AN APOLOGY TO JOAN BAEZ

It may well be the first time
that crystal ever pierced the steel.

in someone's shadow

A NEW LIST OF SAINTS
FOR THE CHURCH OF ROME

Despite St. Valentine's full quiver
his arrows make no mark.
He's been unmasked as Indian giver
in matters of the heart.

St. Nicholas is optional
you'll be pleased to know,
giving gifts is still permissible
as is plastic snow.

Could be we need a few new saints
to help us keep our place.
What about *St. Stokely*
for stirring up his race.

All Saints' Day would be amiss
without *St. Hershey's* letter.
Killing little boys I guess
will make the whole world better.

And now that good St. Chris is gone
who'll prevent the crashes?
St. Nader with his pen in hand
makes Ford break out in rashes.

St. Syntex doth control the fate
of people everywhere.
The Church of Rome is prone to wait
to canonize or care.

St. Hoffa's now a monk they say.
To him the faithful seldom pray.
Don't forget *St. Doctor Spock*
and *St. Joplin* queen of rock.

St. Reagen's good at chopping trees.
St. Union oils our oceans.
St. Leary's literary teas
are tops in campus notions.

To crown this list of new-found saints
and make it everlasting,
St. Portnoy for our sex complaints,
St. Warhol for type casting.

AN EVENT OF SOME IMPORTANCE

I started up the hill
and there they were.
One of them was hardly twenty,
        the other maybe more.

They were still.

Dead I knew.

I slowed but didn't stop.

A cop was waving traffic past.
No ambulance had yet arrived
but two police cars kept a guard
on the coroner's new dibs.

One bike was halfway up a wall
        the front wheel still spinning.
The other, folded over like a half-left sandwich,
grew like sculpture in the middle of the road
and blossomed with the red of one of them.
I didn't know which one.

Looking back
from further up the hill
I saw one cop strike up some flares.
Still no sirens in the distance.

Traffic now crawled up behind me
slowly till we hit Mulholland
and the other side.

Down below was Christmas
as it always is.
Searchlights.
Perhaps a used-car lot
      was opening
or another shop
with shiny motorcycles.

The evening paper
in the driveway once again.
I picked it up
before I parked the car.

Inside
I sat down with a cup of coffee
and wrote a poem on what it's like
to miss a falling star.

Perhaps I should have made a wish
on one of many searchlights,
biting at the clouds.
More dependable than stars
        in California.

A MESSAGE FROM THE FRONT

I don't think we can hold
the chemistry lab much longer
we're running out of Dixie cups
            and Baby Ruths.

We'd better call up Colonel Sanders for reinforcements.
How do you spell Minnie Pearl?

We can't get channel four.
What the fuck do they expect from us,
Ralph Williams sells the same cars
            every hour.

Tomorrow when we give the dean
his bloody nose
our reputations for this year
will finally be secure.
But tonight, because of our commitments,
we've missed Beach Blanket Bingo on the Late Show.
War is hell.

A WORD FROM THE SPONSOR

How tall we are.
We've learned so much.
Everything, it seems,
but how to stay in touch.

in someone's shadow

TEN SONGS

for Wade Alexander

PEOPLE ON THEIR BIRTHDAYS

People on their birthdays will take a drink or two
and tell you how they won the prize in nineteen forty-two,
some other Sunday before the swing came down
and papa smashed the car up on his way in from the town.

People on their birthdays all live in yesterdays
before the kids grew up and went their own ambitious
ways,
wasn't it something that long-ago July
and that's about the time birthday people start to cry.

Happy Birthday, drink a toast to me.
I'm all of ten and goin' on a hundred twenty-three.

People on their birthdays are fond of looking back
to half-remembered yesterdays when things were not so
                                                    black.
Some other summer when playin' ball was fun
and life's rewards were chocolate bars and nickel bubble
                                                    gum.

Happy birthday, one more toast to me.
The race is nearly over
And we can come in free.

People on their birthdays should have a chocolate cake
and be prepared tomorrow for a memory bellyache.
Looks like a rainstorm beyond the cloudy sky,
now birthdays come so often I've forgotten how to cry.

in someone's shadow

SOME TRUST IN CHARIOTS

There were those who must have thought us mad
spending all that time and money we never had.
Well, some trust in chariots and some in marble banks,
some of us just love each other and never ask for thanks.

There were those who must have thought us daft
from the way we cried together and the way we laughed.
Well, some trust in chariots and some in big machines,
some of you save diamonds, baby, some of use save dreams.

Some trust in chariots with great big yellow wheels.
Well, I had a ride in a chariot and oh how empty it feels.

There were those who must have thought us fools
loving like a house on fire and breaking all the rules.
Well, some trust in chariots, in chariots they ride,
we ride the wings of love together side by side.

in someone's shadow

for Jay Foster

ALAMO JUNCTION

When I get back to Alamo Junction
I guess they'll all be pretty surprised
to find out just how tall I've grown
and oh how worldly wise.

When I go home to Alamo Junction
I'll look those people straight in the eyes
the ones who thought I'd never go nowhere
and never come home with the prize.

I'll tell them all what kind of a world
lies beyond the trees.
I'll tell them all of the times I've had
while hiking the highway and sailing the seas.

When I go home to Alamo Junction
they'll all turn out decked out in their best,
they'll welcome me their soldier of fortune
who's set apart from the rest.

When I got back to Alamo Junction
the town somehow just wasn't the same,
All the folks I thought would remember
had all but forgotten my name.

for Novella Nelson

CHILDREN ONE AND ALL

Some of us live in big white houses,
some of us live in small.
Some of our names are written on blackboards,
some are written on walls.

Some of our daddys work in factories,
some of them stand in line.
Some of our daddys buy us marbles,
some of them just buy wine.

But at night you can't tell Sunday suits
from tattered overalls.
Then we're only children,
children one and all.

in someone's shadow

Some of us take our lunch in boxes,
some in paper sacks.
Some of us kids join in the laughter,
some hear it at our backs.

Some of our mothers sew fine linen,
some can't sew a stitch.
Some of our mothers dress up poorly,
some of them dress up rich.

But at night you can't tell party dresses
from hand-me-downs too small.
Then we're only children,
children one and all

Some of us learn our lessons poorly,
some of us learn them well.
Some of us find an earthly heaven,
some of us live in hell.

Some of us go right on a-preachin',
without makin' too much sense.
Some of us hide behind a wall,
some behind a fence.

But at night you can't tell picket fences
from bricks that tower tall.
Then we're only children,
children one and all.

Some of us grow up tall and handsome,
some of us grow up plain.
Some of us own the world in ransom,
some of us just our name.

Some of our people die in mis'ry,
some of them die in peace.
Some of our people die for nothing,
but dying doesn't cease.

And at night you can't tell fancy coffins
from boxes in the hall.
Then we're only children,
children one and all.

BEND DOWN AND TOUCH ME

Bend down and touch me with your eyes.
Make every morning hold a new surprise,
then when I stumble from my sleep
yours is the first face that I'll see.

And as I amble through the day
be there to guide me all along my way.
If I should falter and fall
your shoulder's near enough to touch.

Follow me from darkness into light
then we'll go back again
through every midnight.

Bend down and touch me with your eyes.
Let every evening hold a new surprise.
So when I tumble into sleep
yours is the last face that I'll see.

for Anne and Glenn Yarbrough

SHE

She was like the snow bird
who comes to peck the crumbs
and when you spread your hand
so quickly flies.
A little like the evening,
a whole lot like the night
and every night at suppertime
I'd celebrate her eyes.

She was like the rainbow
you find hard to believe,
changing moods and faces
all the time.
A little like the morning
a whole lot like the day
and every day I'd thank the skies
that she was mine.

in someone's shadow

She could cry and make you feel ashamed
and yet you'd have to burst with pride
because she shared your name.

She was like the willow
that stands below the hill
and calls no man her master
but the day.
A little like a woman,
a whole lot like a child
as children do she changed her mind
and one day went away.

for Robert Fryer

THE IVY THAT CLINGS TO THE WALL

Here on the far side of time
we're near the end of the line.
Our days have grown withered and small
like the ivy that clings to the wall.

Off on the long road to home
we're meant to go it alone,
still there are times we recall
the ivy that clings to the wall.

We hurriedly ran from the safety of schoolyards
in search of a better more beautiful world.
One day we turned in the road to find
our new worlds were all in our minds.

Some other season perhaps
pretty girls sat on our laps.
But seasons can change after all
like the ivy that clings to the wall.

for Greta Keller

ONCE I LOVED

Once I loved the wind as it blew
down from the mountains over the land.
Once I loved the touch of the sun
almost as much as the touch of a hand.

And once I loved the smell of the sea,
the feel of the waves rolling over me.
Sea and sand, air and sky,
Once I loved, once I loved.

Once I loved all of God's things
that grow on the earth and cover the land.
Air and sky, sea and sand,
Once I loved but never till now.

SOMETHING MORE

He'd walked all the roads there were to walk
and some there never was.
He'd asked two and twenty questions
never learning the because.
And he knew that his life would not be
what it was before.
Still he knew that there must be something more.

He'd seen all the towns there were to see
in countries old and new.
He'd done half the things that young men
half his age were wont to do.
He'd walked meadow, hill and highway
knocking once on every door.
Always looking, seeking, needing something more.

As a young man he grew skyward
and tall as any tree.
He was strong of muscle, wide of will,
as young men ought to be.
His young eyes had left the apple
fastened on the core.
For he knew that there must be something more.

Still firm of frame though forty
he awoke one day to find
that the crimson flower of madness
had blossomed on his mind.
And the wind of constant wanting
had in secret won the war.
Still he prayed that there might be something more.

in someone's shadow

And the fine sun of fifty
saw him dying and alone.
Just a man struck down suddenly
by something not yet known.
Just a man who spent all his life
hoping once to soar.
And all the while expecting something more.

Are we all then like that young man
who wanted so to fly?
Who gave his life pursuing life
and daring to ask why.
Daring death to walk beyond the ground
that had been walked before.
Expecting to be offered something more.

God, but there must be something more.

I'LL CATCH THE SUN

I'll catch the sun
and never give it back again.
I'll catch the sun
and keep it for my own.
And in a world where no one understands
I'll take my outstretched hand
and offer it to anyone

who comes along and tells me
he's in need of love.
In need of hope or maybe just a friend.
Perhaps in time I'll even share my sun
with that new *anyone*
to whom I gave my hand.

about the author

ROD McKUEN was born in Oakland, California, and grew up in California and Nevada, Washington and Oregon. He worked as a laborer, cowboy, radio disk jockey, newspaper columnist, and as a psychological warfare script writer during the Korean War, before becoming a best-selling author, composer and entertainer.

Mr. McKuen is the composer and lyricist of the motion picture scores for *The Prime of Miss Jean Brodie* and *Joanna,* and he has written the lyrics to Henry Mancini's score for *Me, Natalie.* In addition, he has just completed the songs for *A Boy Called Charlie Brown,* the first film based on Charles Schulz's comic strip. Mr. McKuen has recorded more than forty albums of his own songs; his more than nine hundred compositions performed by other artists have sold a total of fifty million records. Frank Sinatra and Glenn Yarbrough are but two of the singers that have devoted entire albums to his words and music.

Stanyan Street and Other Sorrows, Listen to the Warm and *Lonesome Cities,* the author's first three books of poetry, have sold nearly two million copies in less than three years, making him the best-selling poet today. He has recently completed a major classical work, *Concerto No. 1 for Harpsichord and Orchestra.*

a note on the type

This book is set in ELECTRA, a Linotype face designed by W. A. Dwiggins (1880-1956), who was responsible for so much that is good in contemporary book design. Although much of his early work was in advertising and he was the the author of the standard volume *Layout in Advertising*, Mr. Dwiggins later devoted his prolific talents to book typography and type design and worked with great distinction in both fields. In addition to his designs for Electra, he created the Metro, Caledonia, and Eldorado series of type faces.

Electra cannot be classified as either modern or old-style. It is not based on any historical model, nor does it echo a particular period or style. It avoids the extreme contrast between thick and thin elements that marks most modern faces and attempts to give a feeling of fluidity, power, and speed.

This book was printed and bound by The Book Press, Inc., Brattleboro, Vermont. Typography by Haber Typographers, Inc., New York. Designed by Andrew Roberts.